JOAN

DONNA KAZ

1 / RESERVATION OF RIGHTS

JOAN © 2001 Donna Kaz

All rights reserved. ISBN-13: 978-1-950201-00-6.

Caution: This play is fully protected under the copyright laws of the United States of America, Canada, the British Commonwealth and all other countries of the copyright union and is subject to royalty for all performances including but not limited to professional, amateur, charity and classroom whether admission is charged or presented free of charge.

Reservation of Rights: This play is the property of the author and all rights for its use are strictly reserved and must be licensed by the author. This prohibition of unauthorized professional and amateur stage presentations extends also to motion pictures, recitation, lecturing, public reading, radio broadcasting, television, video and the rights of adaptation or translation into non-English languages.

Performance Licensing and Royalty Payments: All rights are administered exclusively by the author, Donna Kaz. No one may perform this play without securing authorization and royalty arrangements in advance from Donna Kaz. Required royalties must be paid each time this play is performed and may not be transferred to any other performance entity. All licensing requests and inquiries should be addressed to Donna Kaz, kaz@donnakaz.com PO Box 2100 New York, NY 10021

Author Credit: All groups or individuals receiving permission to produce this play must give the author(credit in any and all advertisements and publicity relating to the production of this play. The author's billing must appear directly below the title on a separate line with no other accompanying written matter. The name of the author(s) must be at least 50% as large as the title of the play. No person or entity may receive larger or more prominent credit than that which is given to the author(s) and the name of the author(s) may not be abbreviated or otherwise altered from the form in which it appears in this Play.

Prohibition of Unauthorized Copying: Any unauthorized copying of this play or excerpts from this play, whether by photocopying, scanning, video recording or any other means, is strictly prohibited by law. This play may only be copied by licensed productions with the purchase of a photocopy license, or with explicit permission from the author, Donna Kaz

Trade Marks, Public Figures & Musical Works: This play may contain references to brand names or public figures. All references are intended only as parody or other legal means of expression. This play may also contain suggestions for the performance of a musical work (either in part or in whole). The author has not obtained performing rights of these works unless explicitly noted. The direction of such works is only a playwright's suggestion, and the play producer should obtain such permissions on their own. The website for the U.S. copyright office is http://www.copyright.gov.

COPYRIGHT RULES TO REMEMBER

1. To produce this play, you must receive prior written permission from Donna Kaz and pay the required royalty. Contact Donna Kaz at kaz@donnakaz.com for written permission.

2. You must pay a royalty each time the play is performed in the presence of audience members outside of the cast and crew. Royalties are due whether or not admission is charged, whether or not the play is presented for profit, for charity or for educational purposes, or whether or not anyone associated with the production is being paid.

3. No changes, including cuts or additions, are permitted to the script without written prior permission from Donna Kaz.

4. Do not copy this book or any part of it without written permission from Donna Kaz.

5. Credit to the author, Donna Kaz, is required on all programs and other promotional items associated with this play's performance.

Have a question about copyright? Please contact me by email at kaz@donnakaz.com.

CAST OF CHARACTERS

JOAN OF ARC/Ensemble.

ACTRESS 1, French History Professor/St. Margaret/French Notary/Ensemble.

ACTRESS 2, St. Catherine/Theologian/Prelate/Ensemble.

ACTRESS 3, Joan's mother/The Dauphin, Charles VII, Earl of Warwick/Ensemble.

ACTOR 1, Joan's Father/Medieval Weapons Expert/Bishop Pierre Cauchon/Ensemble.

ACTOR 2, St. Michael/French Soldier/Inquisitor of the Faith/Ensemble.

AUTHOR'S NOTES

The movement is an intrinsic part of this play and helps to tell the story and move the action forward. It is important to establish an ensemble during rehearsals that will work together to create the scenes of this piece that do not contain text. Slow, almost dance-like movement, combined with music and lighting are essential ways the actors establish mood and telegraph the story prior to each written scene. It is important to balance the use of this technique between dramatic battle scenes and the other dramatic scenes of Joan's life with the element of joy and fun within the play. While the movement can be an honest way to portray battles, it should also be used to tap into the comedy and bliss that Joan must have felt as a teen who fully embraced what she became when she listened to her heart.

MUSIC: Directors of *JOAN* should work with a sound designer to choose music appropriate to each scene. Original music may be written specifically for the piece or prerecorded music/sound can be used but keep in mind that sound recordings are under copyright.

3 / JOAN - PLAY

AT RISE:

An empty space with audience seated on three sides. The playing area is defined with a rope placed on the floor. Inside the square there are 6 large, heavy duty black rubber containers that will be moved by the actors and used for all set pieces.

LIGHTS UP:

MUSIC. The ENSEMBLE walks slowly into the playing space. In slow movement they circle each other. Soon they begin to bump into each other and this leads to fighting. They form a circle and one by one, each actor is thrust into the center while the others taunt them. Eventually one actor cannot escape, is pounded to the ground and raised up by the others. All let out a sound as they collapse onto the floor. Lights change. The SOUND OF BELLS. The ensemble begins to slowly come back to life, each whispering one of their lines from the play. They rise and search the playing area while their voices get louder and louder. Eventually they are shouting one sustained vowel sound together. LIGHTS CHANGE. MUSIC: French. The ensemble changes the set into a class room.

ACTRESS 1/FRENCH HISTORY PROFESSOR:

A brief history of France!

(*The ensemble creates a class of third graders. They react joyously when they hear what their lesson will be*)

The Kings of England have always claimed France. In 1337 the Hundred Years' War begins. Now the Hundred Years' War means that for a hundred years the Kings of England attempt to unite France and England under one crown—their own. In May 1420 a treaty between the French and the English is signed. The treaty states that 1) Henry V of England will take the title of regent and heir of France. 2) Henry V will marry Catherine, the daughter of the French King Charles VI. And 3) the son of King Charles, the Dauphin, will have no say at all in the affairs of France and be declared a bastard.

(*All react with shock. They rise and act out the following*)

June 1420. Henry V marries Catherine of France.

August 1422. Henry dies.

October 1422. Charles VI dies as well.

Henry V and Charles VI each leave a son. Henry VI, a baby 9 months old and Charles, the Dauphin, now 19. According to the treaty, Henry VI, an infant, is recognized as King of France and England and the Dauphin is excluded from his succession to the French throne. France divides into two parties—The

Burgundians and the Armagnacs. The Burgundians support the English.

(BURGUNDIANS *improv some "English" lines such as "Would you like a cooked breakfast?"* or *"Fancy a cuppa?"* or *"That's rubbish!"*)

The Armagnacs become the Nationalist Party.

(ARMAGNACS *improv some "French" such as "Oui, oui!"* or *"Comment allez-vous?"* or *"Excusez-moi!"*)

The French fight the English!

(MUSIC: *French and English battle/dance as PROFESSOR holds up cards which denote the passage of time*:)

2 years! 14 years! 53 years! 87 years!

(*Eventually All are exhausted and die*)

June 1424. Joan, a peasant girl, hears her voices for the first time. She is told that she will solve the problem between the French and the English. She is 13 years old.

(LIGHTS CHANGE)

ST. CATHERINE: Joan! This is Saint Catherine speaking. You are destined to lead a different kind of life!

ST. MICHAEL: Joan! Your main man Saint Michael is speaking to you! You will accomplish miracles!

ST. MARGARET: Saint Margaret here, Joan! You have been

chosen by the King of Heaven to restore Charles to the throne of France!

CATHERINE: You shall put on masculine clothes.

MICHAEL: You shall bear arms and become the head of the army.

MARGARET: France shall be guided by your counsel.
MICHAEL: Give me a J! **CATHERINE & MARGARET:** J!

MICHAEL: Give me an O!

CATHERINE & MARGARET: O!

MICHAEL: Give me an A!

CATHERINE & MARGARET: A!

MICHAEL: Give me an N!

CATHERINE & MARGARET: N!

MICHAEL: What's that spell?

CATHERINE/MARGARET/MICHAEL: Joan! Joan? Joan? Joan?! JOAN!? JOAN!? JOOOOOAAAN!

JOAN: Yes?

MARGARET: You have been chosen by the King of Heaven to

restore Charles to the throne of France.

JOAN: What?

CATHERINE: You shall put on masculine clothes!

MICHAEL: You shall lead an army.

JOAN: Are you sure you have the right person?

(LIGHTS CHANGE. MUSIC. MOVEMENT: The joy of country life. Joan's country home.)

MOTHER: Joan! Joan, come home this instant! Joan, if you are not here by the time I count to ten you are grounded young lady. And don't think I won't do it. One. Two. Three. Four. Don't push me. You know not to push me. Five. Six.

You're pushing. Seven. Eight. Joan, I'm getting a headache. Nine. JOOOOAAAANNNNN!

JOAN: I'm here mother.

MOTHER: Just in the nick of time, as always. Where have you been?

JOAN: In the woods.

MOTHER: What? I told you never to go in those wood. Last year they found a dead dog in there. You don't know what's in those woods...

JOAN: Mother, I heard voices. Saint Michael, Saint Catherine and Saint Margaret spoke to me. They told me that God wants me to help save the Kingdom of France.

MOTHER: What kind of books are they making you read in school?

JOAN: I heard the voice of God, Mother.

MOTHER: Yes? Did He tell you that you should milk the cow?

JOAN: I don't know what to do!

MOTHER: I'll tell you what to do. Go and milk the cow. And don't tell you father you were in the woods. You know how he...

(FATHER enters.)

FATHER: Joan! Where have you been? You're always going off somewhere. Last night I dreamt that you ran off with a band of soldiers.

JOAN: Father, I have been in the woods. And there I heard the voice of God. He wants me to put on men's clothes and restore Charles to the throne.

FATHER: That's very nice, Joan, but did God happen to tell you how we are to escape being attacked by the Burgundians?

JOAN: No.

FATHER: Then what good is he? Next time tell him to tell you something useful.

MOTHER: You didn't really hear anything did you Joan?

JOAN: I did! I heard the voices of the saints. They told me that I must lead an army!

FATHER: That's enough! You keep talking like that and you won't be allowed out of this house!

MICHAEL: Don't listen to him Joan.

JOAN: Did you hear that?

MOTHER: Now listen to me. Go milk the cow right now young lady.

CATHERINE: Forget the cow. Listen to us!

JOAN: I am listening to you.

MOTHER: Good.

MARGARET: You must leave home. You must save France.

JOAN: I must save France!

FATHER: Fine, fine. Just do it after you milk the cow.

CATHERINE: Go to France, Joan.

MOTHER: Set the table. Supper will be ready soon.

FATHER: Milk the cow. And don't run off again.

CATHERINE: Run, Joan.

MARGARET: Go to France.

JOAN: Now?

FATHER: Now, tomorrow and the next day! See that you do your chores and don't be late for supper.

(JOAN, MOTHER and FATHER FREEZE)

CATHERINE: Her father and mother watched her closely after that day.

MICHAEL: She did not go to France for three years.

MARGARET: Finally, she could not put if off any longer.

(LIGHTS CHANGE. The woods.)

CATHERINE: Come on, Joan.

MICHAEL: Let's go, Joan.

MARGARET: Move it, Joan!

JOAN: Shut up!

MICHAEL/CATHERINE/MARGARET: What?

JOAN: I'm sixteen. Leave me alone.

CATHERINE: Oh no, no, no, no, no. Vaucoulers is the nearest town held in the name of the Dauphin.

MARGARET: Go and visit your uncle there.

MICHAEL: From there find an escort into France.

JOAN: You've got the wrong person.

MICHAEL/CATHERINE/MARGARET: We've got the wrong person not!

CATHERINE: You are destined to lead a different kind of life.

MARGARET: Listen up, girlfriend.

JOAN: Me?

MARGARET: You see anybody else here? Yoo hoo! Focus!

JOAN: But I'm a peasant girl!

MICHAEL: Yeah, so? You will accomplish miracles!

MARGARET: You have been chosen by the King of Heaven to restore Charles to the throne of France.

JOAN: You've made a big mistake.

CATHERINE: You shall put on masculine clothes.

MICHAEL: You shall bear arms and be the head of the French Army!

JOAN: Please go away.

CATHERINE: You shall put on masculine clothes.

MARGARET: France shall be guided by your council.

JOAN: This is a mistake!

CATHERINE: You shall put on masculine clothes!

MICHAEL: Check this out. You shall lead an army.

JOAN: But I don't want to lead an army!

MARGARET: You have been chosen by God, honey!

JOAN: Guess he's got to choose somebody else.

MARGARET: Wake UP! Do you want to stay here and milk the cows?

MICHAEL: Or do you want to do something!

CATHERINE: You shall put on masculine clothes!

MICHAEL: You will, like, be remembered for all time.

CATHERINE: You shall put on masculine clothes...clothes of masculinity!

JOAN: Stop saying that!

MARGARET: Wake UP! WAKE UP! Do you really, really want to stay here and milk the cows?

MICHAEL: You will, like, really, really be remembered for all time.

CATHERINE: You shall put on... COMFORTABLE clothes! (Joan's Mother and Father enter.)

FATHER: Joan? Where are you? Did you milk the cow?

MARGARET: You could stay in these totally boring fields forever.

MOTHER: Joan? Joan? JOOOOOOOAAAAAAANNNN!

MICHAEL: Or you could accomplish something really cool.

FATHER: Joan, I've been thinking. Soon you'll be at the age where most young girls get married.

CATHERINE: Choose, Joan. Marriage?

MOTHER: Joan, did you milk the cow?

MICHAEL: Choose, Joan. Cows!? Or action!

(Saints urge Joan to choose. Mother and Father urge her to milk the cow and get married until...)

JOAN: ALRIGHT! I'll do it! I'll save France! (Saints celebrate. Mother and Father turn away.)

MICHAEL/CATHERINE/MARGARET: We shall be with you to help you.

JOAN: What do I do? How do I begin? When do I go?

MICHAEL/CATHERINE/MARGARET: You. You. You. You go now!

(LIGHTS CHANGE. MUSIC: Women change into male clothing. MUSIC CHANGES. MOVEMENT: The walk to Vaucoulours.)

JOAN: Stop! Is this Vaucoulers?

ALL: Yes!

JOAN: The Kingdom of France is not the Dauphin's but my Lord's. My Lord wills that the Dauphin be made King of France. Though I wear my legs to the knees on the road, I shall see the king crowned.

(LIGHTS CHANGE. MUSIC plays under MOVEMENT: a battle scene. LIGHTS restore.)

ACTRESS 3: In 1428 the English began to lay siege to Orleans. The war was deadlocked. Charles held France south of the Loire River, while Henry held the north.

ACTOR 1: There is no record of what Joan looked like. The only certain aspect of her physical being is that she was a virgin.

JOAN: My voices instructed me. I must remain a maid.

ACTOR 2: January, 1429. Joan, aged 17, leaves her home town forever.

ACTOR 1: She arrives at Vaucouleurs and asks the commander of the army to send her to the king.

JOAN: I am Joan the maid. Send me to the King.

ACTOR 1: At first he laughs. Until he recalls the prophecy that said that France would be saved by a virgin.

ACTOR 2: He give her a sword, a horse and an escort.

ACTRESS 2: Joan, who never road a horse before, rides like a master.

(JOAN gets on her horse, ALL follow on their own mounts. She skillfully gallops to the King while ALL try to keep up. MUSIC)

ACTOR 2: She arrives at the King's castle in Chinon.

ACTRESS 3: She has gained the confidence of the men in her company. **ACTRESS 1**: Not one of them lays a finger on her.

ACTRESS 2: She is talked about in the towns.

ACTOR 1: So far she has accomplished...nothing! Joan requests a meeting with the Dauphin. For two days he sends messengers to interview her.

JOAN: I shall only speak to the Dauphin.

ACTRESS: Finally, the Dauphin agrees to see her. On her way into the castle a man yells out...

ACTRESS 2/MAN: Is that not the maid? Why if I had her for one night she wouldn't be the same! Ha!

JOAN: Why do you deny God when you are so near death?

ACTRESS 2/MAN: Near death. Why I'm just a young lad... (Man dies.)

ACTRESS 3: Joan enters the castle. The Dauphin attempts to conceal himself.

(DAUPHIN puts the crown on someone else and seats her on the throne. JOAN knocks on the door.)

ALL: Who eez it?

JOAN: I am Joan the Maid. I am here to see the King!

ALL: Entres!

(At first JOAN kneels at the feet of the imposter but suddenly gets up and picks the DAUPHIN out of the laughing crowd. She kneels at the Dauphin's feet.)

JOAN: The King of Heaven sends me to you with the message that you will be crowned King in the town of Reims.

ACTRESS 3/DAUPHIN: It is not I who is King.

JOAN: I know it is you.

DAUPHIN: Leave us! (*All but Joan and Dauphin sit on the side*:) Why are you here?

JOAN: I come directed by God.

DAUPHIN: How do you know it is God who directs you?

JOAN: He told me.

DAUPHIN: When?

JOAN: When I was thirteen.

DAUPHIN: How old are you now?

JOAN: Seventeen.

DAUPHIN: And you still believe it?

JOAN: Yes.

DAUPHIN: Good for you.

JOAN: God will give you back your kingdom. You will be crowned at Reims.

DAUPHIN: Prove it.

JOAN: Give me an army and I shall.

DAUPHIN: How do I know you won't turn on me? How do I know you will not use the army against me.

JOAN: Charles, you must put your faith in God.

DAUPHIN: Who are you to tell me such a thing? I'll tell you who you are. You're nothing. A peasant girl! You don't know how to read or write. You have no money. You're a girl dressed up to look like a boy. You have no strength for battle. Quite frankly, you're weird.

JOAN: Please listen to me. I have come to make war on the English. I will lead the battle of Orleans.

DAUPHIN: That is the most ridiculous thing I have ever heard.

JOAN: I need soldiers.

DAUPHIN: Why don't you ask God for them?

JOAN: God would give them to me, if this were his kingdom. But is your kingdom.

DAUPHIN: It is not mine, it is Henry's Kingdom!

JOAN: It is the Lord's and the Lord wishes you to be made King.

DAUPHIN: You just said that it is not God's.

JOAN: It is one and the same. God is for you Charles.

DAUPHIN: Why can't he tell me that himself? Why does he need you to come here and tell me?

JOAN: I do not question. I only do as I'm told.

DAUPHIN: Then go away.

JOAN: I cannot. I must lead your army and drive the English out of France. I must bring you to be crowned at Reims.

DAUPHIN: You expect me to trust you just like that? Did you trust your voices from the very beginning?

JOAN: Yes.

DAUPHIN: Why?

JOAN: I did not trust them at first. I did not do what they told me right away. But I always knew that they were from God.

DAUPHIN: How?

JOAN: I don't know. You just know things like that.

DAUPHIN: I don't. I don't trust anything.

JOAN: You believe in God.

DAUPHIN: Of course I do.

JOAN: Then give me your army.

DAUPHIN: Let me think about it. Go away.

JOAN: I don't blame you for not trusting me. It's just that there is nobody in all the world who can recover the kingdom of France except me. Believe me, I would rather have remained at my mother's side, for it is not my nature...yet, I must go and I must do this thing because my Lord will's that I do it.

DAUPHIN: He wills you through your voices?

JOAN: Yes.

DAUPHIN: Let me hear these voices. Tell them I wish to speak to them.

JOAN: I cannot do that.

DAUPHIN: Why not? I am the King. God certainly will speak to me.

MARGARET: I'll speak to you.

MICHAEL: No.

CATHERINE: Why not? It would be cool to speak to the Dauphin.

MICHAEL: Because I said no.

CATHERINE: Oh, get over yourself already. Hey, Dauphin!

MICHAEL: Stop that.

MARGARET: Yoo! hoo! Dauphin. Can you hear us?

CATHERINE: Listen and you will hear.

MICHAEL: That's enough.

CATHERINE: Since when are you in charge?

MARGARET: Yeah, just because you're an archangel doesn't mean you can tell us what to do.

MICHAEL: Come on. Let's not get into this again. (*Saints argue loudly.*)

JOAN: Please be quiet!

DAUPHIN: Who are you talking to? It's them, isn't it. Where are they? How come I can't hear them?

CATHERINE: Because you don't know how to listen.

JOAN: Let me handle this.

DAUPHIN: Where are you? Speak to me!

MARGARET: We are standing right beside you.

CATHERINE: Listen and you will hear!

MICHAEL: He can't hear you. It's no use.

DAUPHIN: I can't hear you.

MICHAEL: When I am right I am so right. Told you.

MARGARET: I can make him listen.

CATHERINE: Me too.

MICHAEL: I won't work. You cannot make anyone listen.

CATHERINE: Oh yeah? Watch this. Hey, Dauphin. Listen up.

MARGARET: Yoo Hoo! Focus, focus, focus. This way. Over here! Listen up! (*Margaret and Catherine try to make the Dauphin hear them:*) OK so I admit you were right about that.

CATHERINE: Now what do we do?

MICHAEL: We are saints, right? We show him a sign.

CATHERINE: A sign?

MARGARET: I get it. Who's got a pen. We'll make it really big. And it can say Saint Margaret...

CATHERINE: And Saint Catherine in red glitter...

MARGARET: And hearts and stars...

CATHERINE: It'll have a big arrow pointing to my name...

MARGARET: And exploding lights and confetti...

CATHERINE: We'll put it up on the side of a church...

MICHAEL: Not a sign, sign. A SIGN!

CATHERINE: We know.

MARGARET: We're on it. A sign.

MICHAEL: Just get behind me. God, I'm a Saint and people don't get what I'm doing. Joan, tell him you will be King.

JOAN: What?

MICHAEL: Just do it, alright? Tell him.

JOAN: I shall be King.

MICHAEL: Good. Now tell him that he doesn't want to be the King.

JOAN: He doesn't want to be the King. I mean, you don't want to be King.

MICHAEL: You will be King instead.

JOAN: I will be King instead.

DAUPHIN: What are you talking about?

MARGARET: Oh, I get it.

CATHERINE: Me too. You are awesome...

MARGARET: So smart...

CATHERINE: I so totally understand why you are an archangel.

MICHAEL: Shhhh...Joan, tell him to listen. (*Saints chant "Lis-*

ten." MUSIC:) **JOAN:** Listen, if you will not agree to allow me to lead your army to battle, then I will be King.

DAUPHIN: You cannot be King.

JOAN: Give me the crown.

DAUPHIN: I will do no such thing.

JOAN: Give me the crown. I will be King.

DAUPHIN: You are not King.

(SAINTS pass the crown from CATHERINE TO MARGARET TO MICHAEL. The DAUPHIN turns just in time to see it float onto JOAN'S head.)

JOAN: I am.

DAUPHIN: How did you do that?

JOAN: As King, I shall give the Kingdom back to He who rightfully owns it.

MICHAEL: Listen.

CATHERINE: Listen.

MARGARET: Listen.

DAUPHIN: Do you hear that?

JOAN: The Kingdom of France is not mine, it is my Lord's.

MICHAEL: We shall be with you to help you.

CATHERINE: We shall be with you to help you.

MARGARET: We shall be with you to help you.

DAUPHIN: Who is that?

JOAN: Whenever I am unhappy, because men will not believe me, I pray to God. And when I have made my prayer to God, I hear voices that say...

M/C/M: We shall be with you to help you. Go, go, go...

JOAN: Listen, Charles. Listen and you shall hear. It is not I who is King. It is the Lord who is King. And the Lord says that you shall be King.

(SAINTS chant. JOAN puts crown on DAUPHIN'S head and leads him to the throne:)

JOAN: Act, Charles and God will act. God give you life, gentle King.

(LIGHTS CHANGE. Ensemble lines up in military formation.)

ACTOR 1: Now! A brief history of medieval weapons. There are two types of long distance weapons: arrows and great balls of stone launched by catapult. Hard stones are used to break down walls and softer stones to crack open skulls. Hand to hand combat is inevitable. Personal protection is very important. Defending your position means building high walls, digging moats and raising towers. From atop these towers men launch arrows and stones at those below. Attacking soldiers try to get over these walls using ladders.

Once inside they fight with swords, lances, maces, and the deadly battle ace which could smash through armor. The French shield is carried not in front of the body but on the back. It looks like a large barrel cut in half and has two leather straps on the inside that the arms can slip through. The wearer can run forward in a stooping position and his entire body will be shielded from attack. At this time half of all the battles are fought hand to hand in small areas. As you have probably figured out, the means of defense are far superior to the means of attack. That is why sieges last so long. Now, does anyone in the audience have a question about medieval weaponry? (At this point Actor 1 can take questions from the audience and ad lib the answers:) Well I see we have a bunch of medieval experts in the house. But let's get back to medieval times where the spirit of the leader...I said the spirit of the leader...is very important. Joan is not a soldier. I said Joan is not a soldier and is ignorant of war. But she believes. She believes. I said SHE BELIEVES and those around her believe because of her.

ALL: Amen!

(LIGHTS CHANGE. MOVEMENT: The battering ram. MUSIC. ALL use slow motion movement to the music suggesting the use of a battering ram to storm a castle. LIGHTS restore.)

ACTRESS 2: The Dauphin decided that in view of the imminent danger to Orleans, Joan would be sent there.

ACTOR 1: Before she was allowed to go she was examined by bishops, doctors and a woman appointed to find out if she really was a virgin.

ACTOR 2: She accepted all these examinations without complaint.

ACTRESS 2: Preparations were made for her to join the army.

ACTRESS 1: She was give an page, two heralds, two servants and her own personal confessor.

ACTRESS 3: As well as a complete suit of armor, a lance, a knife, a battle-axe, a sword, a flag and a standard bearing the image of Christ.

ACTOR 1: The standard was made by Hamish Power, a Scotsman living in France at the time.

ACTOR 2: (In a bad Scottish accent:) "I'll make a standard for you, Lassie!"

ACTRESS 1: The standard is white satin painted with golden lilies and a representation of Christ seated on a globe.

ACTOR 2: Joan was not actually in command of the army. But she made each soldier go to confession and decreed that all their loose women should be left behind.

ACTRESS 2: By April, 1429, Orleans had been under attack for 6 months.

ACTRESS 1: The French were shut up inside the town which was entirely surrounded by walls.

ACTOR 1: The English guarded the north, west and south, but left the east unguarded.

(ALL create the banks of the Loire River and make sound effects of wind.)

ACTRESS 3: Orleans was to the north of the Loire river. The French army had two choices—they could approach the city on the north side, which would allow them to do so without having to cross the river; or they could approach from the south side, crossing over the river. The commander of the army chose to approach from the south. The wind was against them.

JOAN: Whose idea was this? Who was it that decided that we should come on this side of the river and not go straight to where the English are?

ACTOR 2/FRENCH SOLDIER: We shall attack from the east where the English are weak.

JOAN: But the wind! It is blowing in the wrong direction. We shall never get across! I have brought you help from the King of Heaven. You told me you were taking me to the English.

ACTOR 2: This is the best way.

JOAN: How are we to get across in this weather?

ACTOR 2: I don't know. Let me think.

JOAN: Now you want to think?! There is no time!

ACTRESS 2: Everybody at that time, or I should say almost everybody, believed in God. In a God who would intervene and make the unexpected happen.

ACTOR 2: Please God, make the unexpected happen.

ACTRESS 2: In other words, everyone believed in miracles.

ACTOR 1: Listen, the wind is dying down.

ACTOR 2: It's a miracle, praise God! Thank you, thank you, thank you.

ACTRESS 3: When the wind shifts, Joan and the army are able to cross the river and enter Orleans. The City rejoices.

ALL: Hurrah!

ACTOR 2: From that moment on the army has hope in her. We are convinced that she was not of men, but from God and it doesn't much matter that the English are in greater strength than us. The first thing Joan does in Orleans is send a letter to the English.

ACTOR 1: She takes an arrow, ties the letter to the end of the arrow and orders an archer to shoot the arrow over to the English. (*Actor 2 shoots arrow.*)

JOAN: Read! It is news! I am the maid sent by God and I call on you to surrender.

ACTRESS 1: No answer. Joan sends a second letter. (*Actor 2 shoots arrow.*)

JOAN: In case you didn't get my first letter I want to tell you that if you do not surrender we shall strike and it shall be seen who is right before God in Heaven!

ACTOR 1: Still no answer. Joan sends another letter. (*Actor 2 shoots arrow.*)

JOAN: You Englishmen you have no right in France! Abandon your forts and go back to your country. I write to you for the third and last time. (*Pause.*) OK, you asked for it!

ACTOR 1: The Battle of Orleans! The French fight the English. Round One. DING!

(ALL divide up and fight. MUSIC. The following is a dance/battle in a comic style.)

ACTRESS 3: The French win round one.

FRENCH: Perrier!

ACTOR 1: The English fight the French. Round two. DING!

ACTOR 2: The English win round two.

ENGLISH: Scones!

ACTOR 1: The French fight the English again! Round three! DING

(At the end only one Englishman is standing. JOAN, confused, holds her sword. The Englishman celebrates winning the battle and accidentally steps into JOAN'S sword, killing himself.)

JOAN: Many have been killed. The English die without the benefit of confession. My soldiers must give thanks to God for the victory won. Confess your sins immediately. If you do not do so, I shall not stay with you any longer. No man is to carry out another assault if he does not first go to confession. Take care that women of ill-fame follow not the army. It is for these sins that God allowed these English to fall. Take care, do as I say. Be always at my side, for tomorrow I shall have much to do, more than I ever had and the blood will flow out of my body above my breast.

(MUSIC. MOVEMENT: Joan is wounded.)

ACTRESS 3: The battle lasted from morning to sunset. Joan, as she predicted, is struck by an arrow above the breast and when she feels herself wounded, she is afraid.

ACTOR 2: A soldier tried to apply a charm to her wound but she will not have it.

JOAN: I would rather die than do a thing which I know to be a sin. I know that I must die one day but I know not when or how or at what time of day. Until then, I will not knowingly do something which I know in my heart is against what God has shown me.

ACTRESS 2: The French win the battle. The bells of Orleans ring out!

JOAN: Charles must now march to Reims to be crowned.

ACTOR 1: July 17, 1429. The coronation of Charles VII. Compared with coronations in the past, the ceremony is threadbare.

(MUSIC. MOVEMENT: The coronation:)

ACTOR 1: I now crown you Charles the VII, King of France.

ALL: Noel! Noel!

JOAN: The will of God has been done. I have brought Charles to his coronation and he has been crowned King of France. Can I go home now?

(MUSIC. MOVEMENT: JOAN lost in the woods. The other actors form a forest and JOAN searches until she is exhausted and falls asleep beneath a tree.)

ACTOR 1: After being crowned Charles disbands his army. (*Saints choose which of them will bring the bad news. Then they wake Joan up.*)

MARGARET: We've got some bad news, Joan.

CATHERINE: You are going to be captured.

JOAN: When?

MICHAEL: We cannot tell you.

JOAN: But I did everything you asked!

MICHAEL: You must take everything as it comes, Joan.

JOAN: I wish to die when I am captured.

CATHERINE: Whatever happens, we shall be with you to help you.

SAINTS: We shall be with you to help you. We shall be with you to help you...

(*SAINTS exit*)

JOAN: Wait!

ACTOR 1: On May 23, 1430 Joan is captured by the Burgundians.

JOAN: No!

(JOAN is captured. MUSIC. ALL stack up the bins and sit JOAN on top. They taunt her saying things like "We have captured the famous witch of France!" JOAN can take it no longer)

JOAN: STOP! (*Joan jumps off the bins.*)

ACTOR 1: No attempts to rescue or ransom Joan are made by King Charles.

ACTRESS 2: In fact, she will never see the Dauphin again.

ACTOR 1: She is locked up in a tower and given three women to care for her.

ACTRESS 1: They try to make her put on a woman's dress but she refuses.

ACTOR 2: After many days she jumps from the top of the tower, a distance of seventy feet.

ACTRESS 3: Some think she is trying to fly and hold this as proof that she is the devil.

JOAN: I was only trying to escape.

ACTRESS 1: Miraculously, she is unharmed.

ACTRESS 3: Joan is moved to the English held town of Rouen. The English agree to let her be tried by the Roman Catholic Church.

ACTRESS 2/THEOLOGIAN: A very brief overview of the Catholic Church.

(*All but JOAN act out the following.*)

THEOLOGIAN: Jesus was born in Bethlehem to Mary and Joseph around 4 BCE, during the reign of Herod the Great.

ACTRESS 1: It's a boy!

THEOLOGIAN: After Jesus' crucifixion and ascension into heaven his disciples wrote down their beliefs as scriptures and preached Christianity, the belief that God came to earth in the form of Jesus Christ.

ACTOR 1 & 2: God came to earth in the form of Jesus! I said, God came to earth in the form of Jesus!

THEOLOGIAN: Christianity developed into two branches, now known as Roman Catholic and Orthodox Churches and later the Reformation gave us a third branch: Protestantism.

ALL: (Ad lib react:) That's cool. Interesting...,etc.

THEOLOGIAN: The Roman Catholic Church began in Rome, claimed Saint Peter as the first leader and called him the first Pope.

ALL: Papa!

THEOLOGIAN: The Catholics believe that baptized people who reject a revealed truth or Church doctrine are heretics. In the Middle Ages the Roman Catholic Church set up the Inquisition, a branch of the Church that was to investigate and root out heresy.

ACTRESS 3: Hey, any heresy in there?

THEOLOGIAN: A person suspected of heresy is given time to confess and absolve herself and failing this, is brought to trial. Torture was often used to obtain confessions. (*Mime torture. All yell, "I confess!"*:) When all else failed to bring a heretic back to believing in Church doctrine, or if a person relapsed after confessing…and by the way, relapsing is very important in our story…

ACTRESS 1: On second though, I don't confess…

THEOLOGIAN: …they were turned over to the secular arm which alone could impose the death penalty.

ACTRESS 1: Joan is captured in the diocese of Bishop Pierre Cauchon.

ACTRESS 3: Cauchon has helped the Burgundians gain control of much of Northern France.

ACTOR 1: He eagerly presides over Joan's trial for heresy, although he is careful to conduct it according to inquisitorial procedure.

ACTOR 2: He is firmly backed by the authority of Henry VI of England.

ACTRESS 2: Joan is held in the Castle Royal of Rouen. Her feet are chained to a block and she is watched day and night by the lowest of English soldiers who torment and mock her.

ACTRESS 3: She is brought before the Bishop and the Inquisitor of the Faith. Also present are one cardinal six additional bishops, thirty two doctors of theology, sixteen bachelors of theology, seven doctors of medicine and three notaries.

ACTRESS 1: She is granted no advocate and not one witness is called to speak on her behalf.

ACTRESS 2: Eight months after her capture her trial begins. (MUSIC: Rachmanioff. MOVEMENT: Set up for trial.)

ACTRESS 3/EARL OF WARWICK: I am the Earl of Warwick and I command the English troops in this town. I am here to represent King Henry VI and the English Kingdom.

JOAN: The English Kingdom does not include France.

ACTOR 1/CAUCHON: Quiet! I am Bishop Pierre Cauchon. Along with the Inquisitor, the prelate and the rest, I represent the Roman Catholic Church and recognize Henry VI as the King of France and England.

JOAN: Are there none here who recognize Charles, The Dauphin, and the kingdom of France?

ALL: No!

CAUCHON: We have a number of reports that you have acted contrary to the Catholic faith. You are accused of heresy. Do you swear to tell the truth, the whole truth and nothing but the truth?

JOAN: I do not know.

CAUCHON: You must swear to tell the truth.

JOAN: Perhaps you will ask me things that I cannot tell you.

CAUCHON: You must promise to be honest in your answers.

JOAN: How can I promise if I don't know what you are going to ask?

CAUCHON: Swear to answer me with the whole truth and nothing but.

JOAN: I will swear that I do not know how I will answer if I don't know the questions.

CAUCHON: Swear to tell the truth!

JOAN: I swear to tell the truth until you ask me something I cannot tell you.

CAUCHON: What can you not tell me?

JOAN: I cannot tell you what has been revealed to me by God.

CAUCHON: You must make some oath.

JOAN: I swear I will tell you all about what I have done since I set out for France.

INQUISITOR: But we know all about that already.

CAUCHON: Let us move on. Please, for the record, state your name.

JOAN: Joan.

ACTRESS 1/NOTARY: Spelling?

CAUCHON: J.O.A.N. Occupation?

JOAN: Savior of France.

WARWICK: You are a peasant!

JOAN: I am honest, sir.

CAUCHON: Do you know why you are here?

JOAN: No.

INQUISITOR: Because you are a devil, not a savior.

WARWICK: You are an enemy to the English and to God.

CAUCHON: You say that you hear voices.

JOAN: I hear the voice of God.

CAUCHON: How do you hear the voice of God?

JOAN: Through the saints that speak to me.

CAUCHON: And when did you last hear these voices?

JOAN: This morning.

CAUCHON: What were you doing?

JOAN: I was asleep. My voices woke me.

CAUCHON: How did they wake you? Did they touch you?

JOAN: Voices cannot touch.

NOTARY: Should I write that down?

CAUCHON: Do you know who the voices are?

JOAN: The voices are Saint Catherine, Saint Margaret and Saint Michael. God speaks to me through them.

INQUISITOR: How do you know it is them?

JOAN: They told me who they were.

INQUISITOR: And you believed them?

JOAN: Don't you believe the saints?

INQUISITOR: Saints cannot speak to people, they can only speak to priests.

CAUCHON: How do you know that it is not devils speaking to you?

JOAN: Because I can see them and they are beautiful.

CAUCHON: What do you think the devil looks like! You think he is ugly and deformed?

JOAN: You mean he's not?

CAUCHON: The devil is often beautiful. That is how he wins souls.

JOAN: My voices are not from the devil.

CAUCHON: How do you know?

JOAN: I answered that question already.

NOTARY: Because they are beautiful.

CAUCHON: In what way? Do they wear clothes?

JOAN: You think God cannot afford clothes?

(*Notary laughs.*)

CAUCHON: When you see them, what part of them do you see?

JOAN: The face.

CAUCHON: Do they have eyes?

JOAN: Yes.

CAUCHON: Do they have ears?

JOAN: Yes.

CAUCHON: Do they have lips?

JOAN: Yes.

CAUCHON: Do they have noses?

JOAN: Yes.

CAUCHON: Do they have shoulders?

JOAN: I think so.

CAUCHON: Do they have elbows?

JOAN: Probably.

CAUCHON: Do they have legs, feet, toes?

JOAN: I don't know.

CAUCHON: How about eyes?

JOAN: You already asked that.

CAUCHON: Do they have kidneys?

JOAN: I'm not sure.

CAUCHON: Thumbs?

NOTARY: Not so fast.

CAUCHON: Do they have thumbs?

JOAN: Yes.

CAUCHON: How many?

JOAN: Two.

CAUCHON: Each or between the three?

JOAN: Each.

CAUCHON: Do they have hair?

JOAN: I do not have permission to tell you that.

CAUCHON: Who gives you permission?

JOAN: I will tell you that in two weeks.

CAUCHON: You will tell me if they have hair in two weeks or who gives you permission in two weeks?

JOAN: I will tell you when I have received permission.

CAUCHON: What will you tell me?

JOAN: What I cannot tell you now.

CAUCHON: Can you tell me now, what you ask permission for?

JOAN: For permission to tell you.

CAUCHON: To tell me have they touched you?

JOAN: Has who touched me?

NOTARY: Wait a minute!

WARWICK: What language do your voices speak?

JOAN: French.

WARWICK: Does not Saint Margaret speak English?

JOAN: Why should she speak English when she is not for the English?

WARWICK: Treason! She is an enemy to the English and must pay for her crimes!

CAUCHON: We must first determine what her crimes are.

PRELATE: She hears voices.

INQUISITOR: She is a witch!

(MUSIC. MOVEMENT. JOAN hears voices. All argue behind her. RESTORE)

CAUCHON: We have a number of reports that you have acted contrary to the Catholic faith. You are accused of heresy. Do you swear to tell the truth, the whole truth and nothing but the truth?

JOAN: I do not know.

CAUCHON: You must swear to tell the truth.

JOAN: Perhaps you will ask me things that I will not tell you.

CAUCHON: You must promise to be honest in your answers.

JOAN: How can I promise if I don't know what you are going to ask?

CAUCHON: Swear to answer me with the whole truth and nothing but.

JOAN: I swear that I will tell the truth until you ask me something that I cannot tell you.

CAUCHON: What can you not tell me?

JOAN: You are tormenting me with questions I have already answered. I request that all questions you are going to ask me tomorrow be given in advance.

CAUCHON: Your request is denied.

JOAN: I should like all the answers I have already give to be read back. **WARWICK:** Denied.

JOAN: I should like to make my confession and hear Mass.

INQUISITOR: Denied.

(MUSIC. JOAN steps forward and prays. ALL freeze behind.)

JOAN: Most sweet God, in honor of your passion I beg you if you love me reveal to me what I am to say to these Church men. I only wish to do your will.

(RESTORE)

CAUCHON: Joan, I am a bishop. I am directed by God.

JOAN: I, too, am directed by God.

CAUCHON: What proof do you have of that?

JOAN: If you say you are directed by God, I believe you. Why do you not believe me?

CAUCHON: The Church must have proof.

JOAN: I went to the Dauphin and gave him a sign from God. He sent me to Orleans, I captured that city and saw that he was crowned at Reims. What more proof do you need?

CAUCHON: What sign did you give the Dauphin to show him that you came from God?

JOAN: I have promised not to reveal that sign to anyone.

INQUISITOR: Then how are we to believe you?

JOAN: By listening to what I say.

INQUISITOR: Then tell us, what was the sign you gave to the Dauphin?

JOAN: I cannot tell you.

INQUISITOR: She makes no sense!

CAUCHON: What if we were to guess what the sign was? Would you tell us then?

JOAN: I suppose it would be alright if you were to guess.

WARWICK: Let's try and guess what the sign was.

INQUISITOR: Give us a hint.

JOAN: It was beautiful and it was good.

WARICK: Was it gold?

PRELATE: Was it silver?

INQUISITOR: Was it a horse?

NOTARY: Was it bigger than a bread box?

JOAN: I cannot tell you anything more.

CAUCHON: Was it a battle ax?

INQUISITOR: Was it a lance?

PRELATE: Was it a suit of armor?

WARWICK: Was it a ladder?

CAUCHON: Was it a knife?

WARWICK: Was it a flag?

NOTARY: Was it a tree?

JOAN: No.

NOTARY: Are we hot or cold?

JOAN: Cold.

PRELATE: Was it something brown?

JOAN: Maybe.

PRELATE: Was it a croissant?

WARWICK: Was it a lock of your mother's hair?

NOTARY: Was it a boot?

CAUCHON: Was it a severed hand?

INQUISITOR: How is a severed hand brown?

CAUCHON: My hand is brown.

JOAN: The sign was not brown.

NOTARY: What color was it?

JOAN: It was many colors.

PRELATE: Was it a Quiche Lorraine?

CAUCHON: It wasn't food!

PRELATE: We don't know that!

INQUISITOR: Was it a wheel of brie?

PRELATE: Was it a baguette?

CAUCHON: God would not choose food as a sign!

WARWICK: What about the loaves and fishes?

CAUCHON: Joan? Was it food?

JOAN: The sign was brought by angels. I shall say no more.

NOTARY: Was it a standard?

PRELATE: Was it a sword?

INQUISITOR: A horse?

JOAN: You already guessed horse.

INQUISITOR: Was it a donkey?

PRELATE: A dog?

WARWICK: Was it wind?

INQUISITOR: Thunder?

CAUCHON: Come on now she said it was beautiful and good. Let's think!

INQUISITOR: Was it a young nun?

JOAN: No.

CAUCHON: Oh give us one more hint!

JOAN: Alright. The sign was carried in by an angel who flew in through the door. The angel then placed the sign on the Dauphin's head.

CAUCHON: A wig!

INQUISITOR: A hat!

WARWICK: A helmet!

PRELATE: A towel!

NOTARY: Lice!

(*All ad lib guessing until...*)

PRELATE: Wait I have it! Was it a crown!

JOAN: Yes! (MUSIC. MOVEMENT: Celebration:) It was the most beautiful crown made of find gold.

ALL: Made of fine gold!

JOAN: It was a sign from God.

ALL: A sign from God!

JOAN: That the Dauphin should be made King of all of France!

ALL: What!

WARWICK: That's a lie!

JOAN: It's the truth.

WARWICK: You are a conjurer!

JOAN: I am called by God!

CAUCHON: Watch what you say, Joan.

JOAN: I speak the truth. I have always spoken the truth. I have not for one hour lied to you or told you anything that the Lord has not told me. I stand by what I have said and will for all time. You can torture me. You can tear me limb from limb. I will not go back on my word.

INQUISITOR: It is clear she is guilty.

JOAN: Of what? Of being honest? Of hearing God?

(MUSIC. MOVEMENT: Joan prays. ALL shift)

CAUCHON: Do you know the bible, Joan?

JOAN: I have heard it read.

CAUCHON: Do you believe it is the word of God?

JOAN: Yes.

CAUCHON: Then, in the bible it is written. "The woman shall not wear that which pertaineth unto a man, neither shall a man put on a woman's garment; for all that do so are an abomination unto the Lord thy God." Deuteronomy 22:5.

JOAN: If it should please God for me to wear women's clothes I would. But it does not.

CAUCHON: Did your God instruct you to put on masculine clothes?

JOAN: Everything I have done, I have done because my voices told me.

PRELATE: Your voices!

CAUCHON: God has written that it is a sin to put on masculine clothes.

JOAN: For the clothes I wear and for the other things I have done, God will bring me to heaven.

INQUISITOR: You God cannot… CAUCHON: God has said in the bible…do you not hear what the bible says?

JOAN: What have clothes to do with a person's soul?

CAUCHON: It is not our job to question the Lord!

JOAN: It is my job to obey when God speaks to me.

CAUCHON: The bible is God speaking to you. The Church is God speaking to you!

JOAN: So are my voices.

CAUCHON: Which would you rather do, wear a woman's dress and hear mass or wear a man's clothing and not hear mass.

JOAN: Promise me that I may hear Mass if I wear a woman's dress and I will answer.

CAUCHON: I promise.

JOAN: Then give me a dress to wear to Mass...and when I come back I will put on the clothes I have now.

CAUCHON: But you are done with your battles. It is no longer necessary for you to wear a man's clothing.

JOAN: I have not done all God wants. When I have, I will take a woman's dress.

NOTARY: Why do you not do as you are told? Do you want to die?

CAUCHON: It is a sin to wear masculine clothes.

JOAN: These clothes do not burden my soul and to wear them does not displease God.

CAUCHON: I have just read from the bible that it does displease Him.

JOAN: Bring me to the Pope. I demand to be taken before the Pope and then I will answer before him all that I ought to answer.

INQUISITOR: It is impossible.

JOAN: Let it be recorded that you pronounced sentence without the Pope.

CAUCHON: The Pope is far away.

JOAN: Bring me to him. I am strong and can travel.

WARWICK: She is stalling. She won't submit to the Pope either.

CAUCHON: Do you believe that the Pope is the head of the Church?

JOAN: Yes.

CAUCHON: If we bring you to the Pope, will you submit to the Church?

JOAN: I have already answered that I submit to God.

INQUISITOR: Then what do you want with the Pope?!

JOAN: I want to answer his questions.

INQUISITOR: With the same answers you have given us, correct?

JOAN: If he asks me the same questions.

INQUISITOR: We have enough. Let us pass sentence.

CAUCHON: We must be sure that she understands the Church. Joan, do you understand that there are two parts to the Church.

JOAN: You mean God's part and your part?

CAUCHON: Yes. No! One part of the Church is in heaven. It is called The Church Triumphant and it is where God, the saints and all the souls that are saved reside. The other part is on earth and that is called the Church Militant. This is where our Holy Father, the Pope, all the clergy, and all good Catholics are assembled. Now the Church Militant is governed by the Church Triumphant. Do you understand?

JOAN: Yes.

CAUCHON: Will you submit to the Church Militant as it has just been explained to you?

JOAN: I submit to the God who speaks to me.

CAUCHON: You have to submit to the Church Militant, Joan.

JOAN: I have no other answer.

CAUCHON: Joan, if you are confused we will give you counsel. Look around and choose any one of us as your advisor. I must warn you that if you do not, you will be in great danger.

JOAN: I wish to give my confession.

CAUCHON: You must first submit to the Church.

JOAN: You yourself have said that the Church and God are the same. I say I submit to God. It is the same. Why do you make difficulties about that?

CAUCHON: Joan, unless you submit to the Church you will be abandoned as heathen.

JOAN: I am only doing what God commands me.

CAUCHON: If the Church abandons you, you will be in great danger. Your soul shall perish in fire. Your body will be consumed by flames.

JOAN: God will not abandon me. God would never abandon me.

CAUCHON: Then come back to the Church, Joan, I will show you the way.

INQUISITOR: It is time for us to pass sentence.

CAUCHON: She does not understand.

INQUISITOR: She understands. This trial has gone on for over a month. We must pass sentence.

CAUCHON: Wait.

JOAN: For what? For a miracle? For me to see the light? I tell you that I have already seen it. Whatever is going to happen to me, I will not say anything different from what I have already said.

CAUCHON: Read back the charges.

NOTARY: Joan, you have said that from the age of thirteen you have heard voices.

INQUSITOR: That is impossible

NOTARY: You have said that you recognize your voices as those of Saint Margaret, Saint Catherine and Saint Michael.

PRELATE: You are not capable of recognizing saints.

NOTARY: You have said that you wear a man's dress by God's command. **INQUISITOR:** In doing so you have condemned yourself.

NOTARY: You have said that you will not submit to the Church.

CAUCHON: Every good catholic must submit to the Church. Therefore we conclude that you are a heretic.

JOAN: As to what I have said and done, I have done it all through God. You can torture me. You can tear me limb from limb. You can show me the fire. I will not go back on my word.

(LIGHTS CHANGE. Marketplace.)

WARWICK: Order a scaffold to be built. Tell everyone to gather there.

INQUISITOR: Ah France! Thou are much abused!

PRELATE: The crowd will taunt you and throw things at you.

INQUISITOR: For thou has adhered itself to the words and deeds of a woman vain and defamed and of all dishonor full.

WARWICK: On top of the scaffold let there be built a stake.

PRELATE: You shall be tied to the stake.

INQUISITOR: It is to thee Joan that I speak. I tell you that you are a heretic. Indeed, your King is a heretic!

JOAN: I say and swear to you, on pain of life, that my King is the most noble of all Christians!

INQUISITOR: "I am the vine and you are the branches. If one branch not abide in me, it must be cut off, cast into the fire and burned."

PRELATE: Call the executioner. Have him make up a crown that bears the word "heretic"!

WARWICK: He will put the crown on your head.

INQUISITOR: It will be a sign. A sign that you are the devil.

PRELATE: Everyone will laugh at you.

WARWICK: The executioner will light the fire.

INQUISITOR: The flames will crackle and grow higher.

PRELATE: You will burn.

INQUISITOR: But you will not die right away.

WARWICK: You will see the smoke rising.

PRELATE: You will begin to feel the heat.

INQUISITOR: But you will not die right away.

WARWICK: First you will burn.

ALL: This is your last chance. / Do what we now ask. / Take what you say back / Or end your life by fire.

(The ensemble may experiment with just saying a few of the words in a rhythm, adding more and more of the chant until finally the words are clear. MOVEMENT accompanies.)

JOAN: I will submit. I deny that I heard voices. Did you hear me? I do not want to burn. I will submit to the Church.

CAUCHON: Will you sign a document saying so?

JOAN: I cannot read or write.

NOTARY: You can draw. Make a circle.

JOAN: I will make the sign of the cross. Can I make my confession? I would like to make my confession. May I now hear Mass? (*Joan signs.*)

CAUCHON: You have pleased God, Joan. You have saved your soul.

JOAN: Now take me to your prison where I shall no longer be in the hands of the English.

CAUCHON: As a limb of Satan you have been severed from the Church.

JOAN: Then where am I to go?

CAUCHON: We now turn you to over the English for justice.

JOAN: To the English!?

CAUCHON: Go back to your cell and live out the rest of your days on the bread of sorrow and the water of affliction so that you may weep for your sins and nevermore commit them.

(MUSIC. MOVEMENT: Women change back into skirts as Cauchon reads Joan's recantation:)

CAUCHON: I, Joan the Maid, recognize the snare of error in which I was held and now know that I am a miserable sinner. Therefore I have, by God's grace, returned to our Mother the Most Holy Catholic Church. In order that it may be apparent that this is not a deception, I do confess that I have grievously sinned in pretending that I have heard the voices of God through His angels, Saint Margaret, Saint Catherine, and Saint Michael. All of my words and deeds contrary to the Church I now take back, because I desire to live in unity with the Church, nevermore departing from her again. Signed with the sign of a cross, Joan.

(JOAN'S cell. SAINTS visit)

JOAN: Are you angry with me?

MICHAEL, CATHERINE & MARGARET: For what?

JOAN: For saying I never heard you.

MICHAEL, CATHERINE & MARGARET: Happens all the time.

CATHERINE: Well, bye Joan.

MARGARET: So long, Joan.

MICHAEL: Later, Joan.

CATHERINE: Don't let your feminine clothes get you down. Where to, Michael?

MICHAEL: I think we're off to Fatima.

CATHERINE: Cool!

MARGARET: I love Fatima.

JOAN: Wait! Are you going to come back?

MICHAEL: We're saints, man, we're always around.

CATHERINE: But we're busy. Working the world, you know?

MARGARET: Besides, the Church says you can't hear us.

MICHAEL: So how you gonna listen? Dig?

JOAN: But I am destined to lead a different kind of life, remember?

MARGARET: You're a peasant girl, Joan.

JOAN: I will accomplish miracles.

MICHAEL: From here?

JOAN: France has been guided by my council.

CATHERINE: That was then.

MICHAEL: This is now.

MARGARET: Time to come up with plan B, you know?

JOAN: I have been chosen by God.

MICHAEL, CATHERINE & MARGARET: Guess he's got to choose somebody else!

(MUSIC underscores)

JOAN: No. I will go back home. I will go back to the woods. I will sit beneath the oak tree...listen! I hear God in the stream, in the wind, in the rock. I feel God standing in the middle of the forest in the heat of the sun on my skin. God runs with me down the hill and God drops his tears on my face when it rains. God calls to me, touches me and pushed me to get up and go! (Saints respond to Joan by repeating the word "Go!") I must finish what I have set out to do. I shall accomplish even greater things than I have already done. I must go to my army and tell them to have faith and not to fall back. In a little while the country will again be ours. Our Lord has condemned the English. In God's name I must fight them. In God's name I must fight them. IN GOD'S NAME I MUST FIGHT! (MUSIC: 1812 Overture. Joan takes off her skirt:) Sound the trumpet and to horse! It is time to rejoin our noble King Charles and fight on. I bring you the finest help that ever was brought to any country for I bring you the help of the King of Heaven. God has commanded me and I will fight!

(Back to JOAN'S cell.)

CAUCHON: You have signed a document saying that you recant and that you will now obey the Church. Why have you put on masculine clothes?

JOAN: I dress this way because it is the way I dress.

CAUCHON: Has anyone told you to do this?

JOAN: I have done it of my own free will.

CAUCHON: Have you heard your voices since you signed?

JOAN: You said that I would be taken out of irons.

CAUCHON: Have you heard your voices?

JOAN: You said I would be allowed to hear Mass.

CAUCHON: Have you heard your voices!

JOAN: Yes.

CAUCHON: What did they say?

JOAN: It doesn't matter what they said All that matters is that they spoke to me. And I can hear them.

CAUCHON: Do you believe the voices are from God?

JOAN: Yes! Yes the voices are God!

(CAUCHON crosses himself and leaves the scene. JOAN hears God and breaks out of her chains. During the speech she is overcome with joy at hearing her voices. MUSIC)

JOAN: God speaks to me. And I would rather die than deny the power inside that voice. I can hear! I am Joan and I hear the voice of God! I have never done anything against God and against the faith. I can hear God above me, below me and inside of me. Isn't it wonderful!?

(JOAN repeats "I can hear. Isn't it wonderful?!" as the ensemble play English soldiers, surround her and burn her at the stake. At the end they let out a SOUND and fall)

ACTRESS 3: The Catholic Church unanimously votes that Joan is a relapsed heretic.

ACTOR 2: She is handed over to the secular arm with a recommendation to be gentle with her.

ACTRESS 3: This is a conventional formula of the Inquisition and everyone knows what it implies.

ACTRESS 1: On the morning of May 30th, 1431 Joan is allowed to give her final confession.

ACTRESS 2: Bishop Cauchon also gives his permission for her to receive the sacraments.

ACTOR 2: They have declared Joan to be a relapsed heretic, yet they allow her to receive the Eucharist.

ACTOR 1: They take her to the marketplace, where ten thousand people have gathered.

ACTRESS 2: She is forced to climb up onto a scaffold. A priest reads from the bible.

JOAN: I kneel down and say my own prayer.

ACTRESS 3: An English soldier hands her a crude cross made out of two pieces of wood.

ACTOR 2: The fire is lit.

JOAN: No one can save me from the pain. I try not to cry but cannot.

ACTOR 1: When it is over, the Executioner says that in spite of all the oil and fuel he used her heart is the only thing that will not burn.

ACTRESS 3: He throws everything which remains of her into the Seine.

ACTRESS 2: Joan's death is followed by an immediate resumption of English military operations.

ACTRESS 1: In 1450 the English are defeated and leave France.

ACTOR 2: In 1456 the verdict in Joan's trial is overturned.

ACTOR 1: May 16, 1920, Joan is canonized a saint by the Roman Catholic Church.

(MUSIC ends)

ACTRESS 2: There are many miracles, large and small that happen on earth.

ACTOR 2: The sun rises and sets, the moon comes and goes.

ACTRESS 3: But one miracle walks on the ground and listens.

ACTOR 1: One miracle hears the voice of God.

ACTRESS 1: One miracle lives and grows old.

JOAN: God's true miracle on earth is all of humankind.

ACTRESS 1,2 & ACTOR 1: Listen.

ACTOR 1,2 & ACTRESS 1,2,3: Listen

ALL: Listen.

(MUSIC. MOVEMENT: listening. Repeat top of play— whispering as if one of JOAN'S voices. ALL freeze)

JOAN: Listen!

(LIGHTS fade to black)

THE END

THE AUTHOR SPEAKS

What inspired you to write this play?

I was hired by a university to direct a production of The Lark by Jean Anouilh. I needed 20 students but only 6 showed up for auditions. I suggested to those 6 students that I would write a modern retelling of the story of Joan of Arc specifically for them. I began researching Joan of Arc and realized that her story really is the story of a rebellious and inspired teenager. The students were very enthusiastic about injecting their own energy and youth into the script. After a 6-week workshop *JOAN* was presented in front of an audience. The world premiere of *JOAN* was produced by TNT Theatre in Scranton in 2000 where it won a Jason Miller Award for Best Production by the Scranton Times.

Was the structure of the play influenced by any other work?

The structure of the play was partly inspired by my circumstances. The first production at the college had no budget for a set designer, costumes, etc. so I worked with what I had which was 6 actors. The cast created each setting via movement using their bodies and voices to invoke changes of scene, tone and atmosphere. The play took on a cinematic quality as we incorporated slow motion, pantomime, parody and even dance to dramatize Joan's life. The minimal technical elements meant that I had to create fluidity within the storytelling via scenes that connected via the actors movements. I trained with the Performance Group and the Wooster group early in my career and was influenced by the way their performances had a coherence because of their use of movement and sound.

Have you dealt with the same theme in other works that you have written?

Yes. I have a touring theatre company, Endurance Theatre, that has toured both the US and abroad. We took *JOAN* to the Edinburgh Festival Fringe in 2001. When you tour you are at an advantage if you can travel light. In my plays the actors are the focus of the theatrical performance.

What do you hope to achieve with this work?

I want audiences to be inspired by Joan's determination and commitment. I also want to give actors the opportunity to work in a true ensemble piece and to be challenged to use all of the elements of performance, i.e. body, voice, emotion, to engage an audience and tell a story. The play is written for 6 actors playing a multitude of roles but it can also be presented using a larger cast.

What are the most common mistakes that occur in productions of your work?

It would be a mistake to not approach the play as an ensemble piece. Also, the use of sound is very important because it is a movement-based piece. Sound must be carefully thought out and incorporated early in the rehearsal process.

What inspired you to become a playwright?

I began as an actress and started writing because of the lack of good material for women that was out there. When I began writing plays I found that I could draw on my training in dance and visual art and incorporate those elements into my work. It is very satisfying to be able to draw upon many different art forms as a playwright.

How did you research the subject?

I researched Joan of Arc and the history of France extensively mostly via books and Joan's own trial transcripts which are well preserved and available. Research was very important in this piece because it is based on history. Every historical aspect in the piece is accurate.

If you could give advice to your cast what would it be?

Work together. Be aware of each other. Enjoy being part of an ensemble and let it inspire your individual work. Have fun. Listen.

How was the first production different from the vision that you created in your mind?

When I am writing a play I do have a specific vision of the finished work but that is always changing based on what happens in the rehearsals. I think that as a writer you must be open to your vision changing constantly throughout the collaborative process. If you are open to let the piece surprise you in the end you will create the piece you meant to create all along.

About the Author

Donna Kaz is a multigenre writer, director and activist based in New York City. For the past 20 years she has led the theatre troupe, Guerrilla Girls on Tour, around the world with performances and talks focused on how to create humorous works which address social issues and prove feminists are funny at the same time. Kaz's memoir, *"UN/MASKED, Memoirs of a Guerrilla Girl On Tour,"* (Skyhorse 2016) was named best nonfiction prose of 2017 by the Devil's Kitchen Literary Festival. Her plays/musicals have been produced around the world including "Stamina" (American Renaissance Theatre/Best Ten Minute Plays of 2019 Smith and Kraus); "JOAN" (Edinburgh Festival Fringe) "Performing Tribute 9/11" (Harlem Stage); "Feminists Are Funny, Pride edition" (Lincoln Center); "The History of Women in Theatre: Condensed" (Women Playwrights International, Dramalabet, Sweden); "Silence Is Violence" (Women's Arts International Festival, Kendal UK) "If You Can Stand the Heat: and "The History of Women and Food" (City of

Women Festival Slovenia). Her awards include a Jerry Kaufman Playwriting Award, Venus Theatre Lifetime Achievement Award, Ian MacMillan Writing Award, Boundary Stone Screenwriting Award, Skowhegan Medal and the Yoko Ono Courage Award for the Arts. She was named a "Notable Woman in American Theatre" by CUNY-TV and has been the Thomas P. Johnson Distinguished Visiting Artist at Rollins College. She has held residencies at Yaddo, Ucross, Blue Mountain, Djerassi, Wurlitzer, Mesa Refuge and Marble House. She has taught and directed at Concordia College, Bloomsburg University, Ursinus College and led workshops on campuses in 48 US States. Her new eBook, *"PUSH/PUSHBACK 9 Steps to make a Difference with Activism and Art (because the world's gone bananas)"* can be found at ggontour.com or donnakaz.com

@donnakaz

Facebook

5 / PRESS

JOAN BY *DONNA KAZ* - **Edinburgh Festival Fringe**

An opening scene of writhing bodies drenched in bombastic classical chords and violent red lights. God, did I want to hate this. But a heartbeat later and I was hooked so what can I say? This is an amazing, brilliant play where every element has come together in perfect alignment.

Written and directed by Donna Kaz, the story avoids epic overkill and goes straight to the heart of the human being behind the myth of France's answer to *Braveheart* – "I'm 16, leave me alone," the young goatherd prudently informs the saintly voices that instruct her to don men's clothes and wage war on the English invaders.

In a vibrant blend of narrative and physical, where the grammar of movement is as complex as the spoken, a flowing series of snapshots chart the warrior maiden's journey to her doom, punctuated by startlingly informative digressions, chorus-like, on dynasties, weapons of war, the Inquisition and the siege of Orleans.

Joan leads a six-strong cast which delivers its multi-roles with hi-energy sensitivity, pushing perfect script and direction even higher.

Oh, and the best techno-medieval soundtrack of the festival.

-Nick Awde The Stage, Edinburgh

VOICES IN HER HEAD

Thanks, but no thanks to Hollywood and TV for handing us two bloated, overdone Joan of Arcs in the past six months. TNT Theatre's *JOAN* gets to the passion of the martyr's story in a way these glitzier productions couldn't.

TNT's *JOAN* will make you sweat. It's raw, physical and bursting with energy. By the end of the 70 minutes show the actors' clothes are wet with perspiration. The show requires them to do a whole lot more than just stand still and deliver lines. The actors are in non-stop motion...dancing, jumping, tumbling their way through the story.

This is how the play works: There are six actors, who each play multiple roles. They wear funky, malleable costumes that change with a few twists and turns to represent the actors' different incarnations. Through a series of vignettes the players tell the story of Joan. The vignettes flow into one another like a live-action montage, switching genres and settings in a flash.

People who have grown up on a steady diet of MTV and Quentin Tarantino films will immediately embrace the jump-cut style of *JOAN*. the moment you think things might start to get boring, the actors transform into new characters and turn the play into a new direction.

Director and writer Donna Kaz uses music that accompanies the action, perfectly segueing from atmospheric melodies to the *William Tell Overture* to an instrumental version of the Beatles' *Eleanor Rigby* and more. Much of the play feels like a highly literate artsy music video. There couldn't be a more ideal play to which to bring a theatre-reluctant teenager. Its also perfect for anyone who likes to be challenged by a non-linear narrative. It's the opposite of often cheesy, humdrum musical theatre.

If you didn't pay attention during European history class, a few of the vignettes capsulate the potentially dry details into entertaining edible snippets that clue the audience in to the political drama Joan dealt with. The two main motifs in Joan's life were battle and the hearing of voices...and the risk of these coming off cheesy in a stage production seemed high. I was nervous that I'd hear ominous, saintly voices piped in from backstage and have to watch painfully fake-looking battle scenes. Kaz handled both elements skillfully and steered clear of obviousness at every point.

The battle scenes were more like dances than anything. As soldiers, the actors moved in slow motion under dimmed red lights in uniquely choreographed fights. They made the battles look sparingly brutal yet entrancing through deliberate movements and facial expressions that hid nothing. Kaz set off these dark, fierce scenes with comic relief from Saints Michael, Catherine and Margaret. The cast as a whole works flawlessly together and moves almost like one seamless being, each aware of what the others are doing even as they move through multiple transitions. The energy they exude transfers directly into the audience

I dare you to walk out of *JOAN* without a tear in your eye and the feeling that you can change the world for the better.

- Anne Marie Deluca, Electric City

Cast of JOAN at TNT Theatre, Scranton PA

Cast of JOAN at Dramaworks

Cast of JOAN at Dramaworks

JOAN - PRODUCTION HISTORY

2017 Lake Taupo School - New Zealand

2016 Dramaworks - Hungary

2012 Fortis Academy, CA

2006 Regis College, MA

2004 Coffeeville Community College, KS

2003 Caxton Youth Theatre, UK

2001 Edinburgh Festival Fringe, UK

2000 TNT Theatre, Scranton, PA